Self-Publishing on Amazon Made Easy

For Print and eBooks

Mike Swedenberg

Mike Swedenberg

DEDICATION

To my fellow writers who made the effort
and published their books.

Contents

"The road to hell is paved with adverbs."
—Stephen King

Forward

The following is my 10-hour lesson plan
presented to Writers at
Nassau Community College, Garden City NY
Queensborough Community College Continuing Education

Parts of my presentation involve classroom participation and reviews of author biographies and their book descriptions. We also experiment with searching tags, discussion of bestseller book covers and demonstrations of uploading books to publish. I have tried to recreate those in this book. If you have a question or a problem, you may email me at mike@swedenberg.com and I will attempt to help you. No charge of course.

Best of luck and keep writing,

Mike Swedenberg

In September 2018, Amazon merged their print service, Createspace with its eBook platform KDP (Kindle Direct Publishing)

While formatting an eBook is different from print, the foundation of self-publishing is the same.

Mike Swedenberg

My Background

Education
Adelphi University BS Business and Management
School of Visual Arts Advertising Copywriting and Design
Gotham School of Writing

Career

Ten years in Advertising Copywriting and Production
35 years in sales for Fortune 50 companies including sixteen years in sales, for global publishing companies
Five years as a Continuing Education Instructor
Self-Publishing since 1996.

Published Works

Study Guides to the US Immigration Test in 12 Languages

Bi Lingual editions available in Print and eBooks:
Spanish, Polish, French, Portuguese, Russian, Bosnian,
Korean, Vietnamese, Chinese, Albanian, Arabic and Tagalog.

Non Fiction

The Sales Rep Survival Guide
The Road Warrior
Advertising Copywriting and the Unique Selling Proposition
21 1/2 Things to Know Before Self-publishing a Book: 2016
Smart Money Stupid Money: 2016

My Total – thus far
29 titles in print, eBooks and one CD with worldwide distribution.

Writers' Corner

In my lectures, I take time to discuss resources that help new writers make their book as good as possible. They usually are dispersed throughout the classes, but I condensed them here for your convenience.

How to become a published author before you publish your first book.

Get your letter to the Editor published in the local paper, submit a short story or poem for publication and be accepted and that makes you a published writer. It adds to your credentials and your by-lines.

MAGAZINES ACCEPTING SUBMISSIONS NOW
WritersMarket.com lists hundreds of magazines for writers of fiction, nonfiction, poetry, writing for children, and more. Here are three magazines with open to submissions now: Antioch Review is open to submissions of poetry until April 30 and essays until May 31. This publication pays $20 per printed page. Potential writers should submit via post with a self-addressed, stamped envelope (SASE).
The Cincinnati Review is open to submissions of fiction, poetry, and nonfiction until April 15. Payment is $25 per page for prose; $30 per page for poetry. Writers should submit by post with SASE or via their online submission system.
The Paris Review is open to submissions year-round for fiction, poetry, and essays. Payment ranges from $75 for poems to up to $3,000 for prose. Writers should submit by post with SASE.
(NOTE: If you're unable to access the listing, it means you need either to log in or sign up for WritersMarket.com first.)

WritersMarket.com lists more than 8,000 publishing opportunities, including listings for contests, magazines, book publishers, literary agents, conferences, and more. Log in or sign up today to start submitting your work.

Subscribe to the free newsletter at <u>http://www.authorspublish.com/</u>

Recent alert
Book Publishers Open to Simultaneous Submissions
Written by Emily Harstone

Source: http://litreactor.com/columns/talk-it-out-how-to-punctuate-dialogue-in-your-prose
Editing tips
If you're writing a novel, you need to be consistent in how you punctuate

dialogue. Copy these examples and keep them handy when you are writing or editing. Given time it will come naturally. Nothing will flag your book as written by a novice like incorrect punctuation.

Note the use of commas and capitalization. Punctuation marks always go inside the quote marks.

Said Mary, "Call me tomorrow."
"Call me tomorrow," said Mary.
"Call me," said Mary, "tomorrow."
"Call me tomorrow," said Mary. "Have a nice evening."
"Call me tomorrow. Have a nice evening," said Mary.
"Call me tomorrow," Mary said. "Have a nice evening."
"Okay," said Frank. "I'll talk to you tomorrow."

Next, let's take away the dialogue tags, which are the words that identify the speaker (said Mary.):
"Call me tomorrow. Have a nice evening."
"Okay, I'll talk to you tomorrow."
                Check your novel for punctuation before publishing it.
                        Above all, be consistent.

If only two characters are speaking, you only need to identify them once. After that, the reader can follow the convesation.

In class, I hand out a worksheet and we practice.
"What time are we leaving," Bill asked.
"I'm guessing around eight," Hank said.
"We can take my car."
"I appreciate it since mine is in the shop."
"What happened?"
"The transmission sprang a major leak."
"That is going to cost you."

Avoid using adverbs and adjectives to emphasize the character's intent. It only serves to slow the reader down and labels you an amateur writer.
Bad
"Well it's about time you showed up," Roger said with exasperation.
"Sorry man," Greg said sheepishly.

Better
"Well it's about time you showed up," Roger said.

"Don't get frustrated every time I'm a few minutes late. I can't help it. I'm an ER doctor," Greg said.

Greg's response sets the table for Roger's frustration without spelling it out to the reader.

The only dialogue tags you need are "said," "asked" and an occasional "replied." Your readers' eyes are trained to skim over them.

Best
Craig Johnson's successful series *Longmire* uses a different method of writing dialog, one without tags. He uses action words to set the scene. It is a technique I have migrated to over the last two years. Here's how he may have handled it.

Roger folded his arms and shook his head. "Well it's about time you showed up."
Greg came to a halt and caught his breath. "Don't get frustrated every time I'm a few minutes late. You know I'm an ER doctor on call."

The reader can see the characters actions in their mind as they hear their conversation. You can use a combination of tags and action words to create your own distinct style.

Google this article in *WritersDigest.com*
47 Things Longmire Author Craig Johnson Taught Me About Writing
By Landis Wade, June 27, 2018

> **If your dialogue is so weak that you need to pretty it up with adverbs, adjectives and unnecessary words, you need to write better dialogue.**

Suggested Reading

If your book isn't well written, and to the standards of the industry, it won't sell.

You need to learn what the Pros look for and how they weed out the inept writers.

By understanding this you can begin your book on the correct path and avoid many of the pitfalls newbies make because they think they can wing it–who think their words are golden and everyone will line up to buy their precious novel, memoir, cookbook or children's book.

**Stephen King On Writing 10th Anniversary Edition
A Memoir of the Craft**

Immensely helpful and illuminating to any aspiring writer, this special edition of Stephen King's critically lauded, million-copy bestseller shares the experiences, habits, and convictions that have shaped him and his work. - Amazon.com

Thanks, But This Isn't For Us by Jessica Page Morrell. A fun, practical guide that reveals the essentials of good fiction and memoir writing by exposing the most common mistakes literary writers make. …these beginners' mistakes drive any agent or editor to their stock rejection letter, telling the aspiring writer "Thanks, but this isn't for us," and leaving many to wonder what exactly it is that they're doing wrong. – Amazon.com

Social Media for Writers by Tee Morris and Pip Ballantine Maximize the Potential of Your Online Brand!

Over the past decade, social media has transformed from a fad into a necessity for writers. But for the inexperienced author, trying to make sense of--much less master--the available platforms can be a frustrating experience. The variety of social media options alone is dizzying enough: WordPress, Tumblr, Facebook, Twitter, Google+, YouTube, Pinterest, and more. – Amazon.com

Story Engineering by Larry Brooks will help you plan out your book to make it work. After reading this, I discovered the hidden mistakes that were holding my novels back. Approach his advice with an open mind and structure your novel rather than flying by the seat of your pants and ending up with a piece of junk no one wants to read.

Class 1 The World of Self-Publishing
"I do not over-intellectualize the production process. I try to keep it simple: Tell the damned story."
—Tom Clancy

Overview

Access to MS Word – no pdf, book publishing software or Open Source
Access to Word Paint or Photoshop for cover design
Social Media for marketing

Objective

To get you published by the end of the semester
BUT
you need something to publish--now get to work

This is a Self Publishing Class…

This isn't a Writing class, HOWEVER--we'll discuss writing skills.
This isn't a Marketing class, HOWEVER--we'll discuss marketing your book.
This isn't a Social Media class, HOWEVER--we will discuss SM to promote your book
This isn't a SEO class, HOWEVER-- ahh the good old Search Engine Optimization mine field.
This isn't a Design class, HOWEVER--you will design your cover and be the Art Director even if you hire someone to do it.
This isn't a Law Class, HOWEVER--there are legal issues you must be aware of when you self-publish.

Self-published authors are now on the
New York Times Best Seller List

INDIE WRITERS RECOGNIZED BY THE NY TIMES

BACK UP - BACK UP - BACK UP
My Horror Story

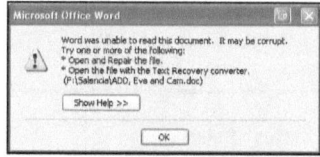

I had just completed an 80,000-word novel, and I thought of one small edit. When I opened the file, I saw the dreaded Error Message: "Word was unable to read this document."

I panicked. I had no backup copy of the completed book. Yes, I had earlier copies, but they were before I had made significant revisions. When I found a way to open the corrupt file, all I saw was code.

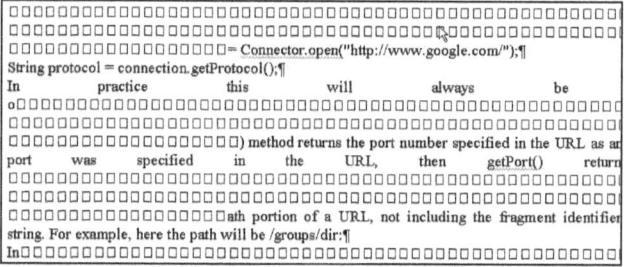

After Googling several resolutions, I cut & pasted the text into Notepad. I then went line for line to delete the code. It was a three-week process.

Now I back up my back up and even email myself a copy. I'll never be more than one day's edits behind.

On another occasion, my Windows 8 crashed. The hard drive was corrupted, and I had to get a new PC. I tried to download another copy of MS Office that I bought online, but I had used my last seat. I'm working on a 28-day trial then had to buy Office again.

A few months later, a virus attacked my external hard drive, and I could not access my files for my classes. Fortunately, I had backed up everything I needed on a thumb drive.

Depending on your computer skills and comfort level, you can back up on the Cloud which allows for redundancy, remote access, backup and the use of convenient mobile devices like smartphones, tablets, laptops with limited storage but excellent portability.

Moral of the story

Back up, back up and then back up your back up. After that, email yourself a copy of the book. That is an easy way to access your book file.

Tasks

Go to Amazon.com Books and find other books in your genre or category you want your book listed under.
An example is Romance.
Within that genre there are sub categories such as:
Action & Adventure
African American
Anthologies
Billionaires
Clean & Wholesome
Contemporary

Find a book on the New York Times bestseller list from a traditional publisher and study the cover design, description and Author Biography.

Find one from an Indie publisher and study.

Find an Indie book (self-publishers are Independents or Indies) that you think needs improvement. What would you would do differently?

Write your book description--approximately 140 words. See Class Three

Write your About the Author–3rd person. See Class Three

Create a Twitter, Pinterest and FB account
Write a tag line for your book. For further information see:

How to Write a Tagline for Your Book (And Why You Need To)
/https://writershelpingwriters.net/2013/09/how-to-write-a-tagline-for-your-book-and-why-you-need-to/

"A tag line is a catch phrase. It doesn't tell you anything specific about the story, but it does give you a feel for it in a way that a logline can't. A tag line is what you see on movie posters."
Lord of the Rings tag line: One ring to rule them all.

The Pros and Cons

Traditional Publishing pros
Source: WritersDigest.com

- Wide distribution and more exposure
- Most offer an advance, sometimes a large one
- They do the editing, formatting, and cover art
- Marketing power

Traditional Publishing Cons

- Take six to eighteen months before publication
- Price ebooks too high
- They have power over cover art and title
- Don't use the marketing power they wield effectively
- Pay royalties twice a year
- Don't involve you in the decisions regarding your book
- Difficult to implement changes
- Low royalty rates, between 6% and 25%
- Very hard to break into the industry

Self-Publishing Pros

- You're paid once a month
- You control price, editing and cover
- Publication is almost instant
- Easy to implement changes
- Every decision is yours
- Great royalty rates
- Anyone can do it

Self-Publishing Cons

- No free professional editing, formatting, or cover art
- Fewer sales
- Less than 10% of current book market – but growing
- Greater potential for poorly crafted books to get published.

10 Reasons Self-Published Authors Will Capture 50 Percent of the Ebook Market by 2020

By Mark Coker Founder, Smashwords
"There's a debate raging about the impact self-published ebooks will have on the book publishing business. By my estimates, self-published ebooks will account for 50 percent of ebook sales by 2020."

Terms You Need to Know

Trade book
A book published by a commercial publisher and intended for general readership. The publisher retains rights to the work.

Indie or Independent Author
The author retains their rights in the work. Either the author publishes in their own name, or sets up a publishing entity to publish, or is part of some co-operative, collaborative or company in which they have a significant input.

eBook or Electronic Book: An electronic version of a printed book like Amazon Kindle and Barnes & Noble Nook.

Open an Account with the following

Independent Publishing with KDP
Kindle Direct Publishing for Print and eBooks

- Free and Easy Tools

- Do-it-yourself and finish fast with tools like Interior Reviewer, Cover Creator, Preview, and Image Gallery.

- Higher Royalties

- Place more in your pocket with some of the best economics in the industry. View Earning Royalties video.

- Comprehensive Book Services

- Get the help you need to complete your book with our affordable design, editing, and marketing services.

- Always Available

- Your work is manufactured to meet demand, so your title is always in stock. There are no upfront costs and no need to carry inventory.

- Wide Distribution Options

- Reach readers for free. Make your book available through Amazon.com, Amazon Europe, your own eStore, Kindle and Expanded Distribution options.

- Help when you need it

- Get answers fast over the phone, by e-mail, or join our Community and discuss your ideas, questions, and more with folks just like you.

The Enrollment Process at KDP.com

Internet Explorer works best

https://kdp.amazon.com/en_US/

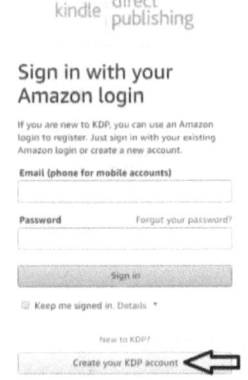

Enter your information

Security Suggestions

Set up a separate email address for your account

JohnsPoetry@google.com

MichelesChildrensBooks@yahoo.com

Complex but easily remembered password

My Tech guy recommends your cellphone number followed by your initials: 2125550002CYOA or no initials and your area code in the middle: 555212002

Setting up a new KDP account.

If you want to get paid, you'll need to fil out the financial information. If you don't, then you can't publish any books.

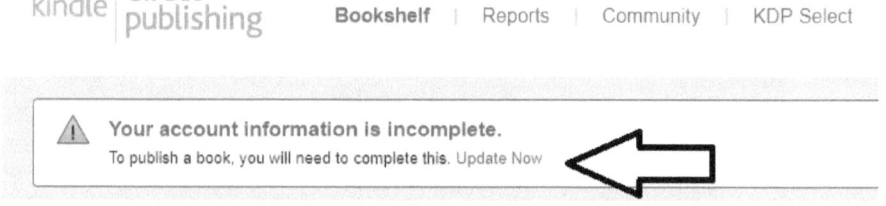

Follow this link to manage your account information, and enter your contact information.

Full Name / Company Name: Unless you're a corporation, enter in your legal name. Do not enter you pen name, if you're using one or several. They will go under this one account.

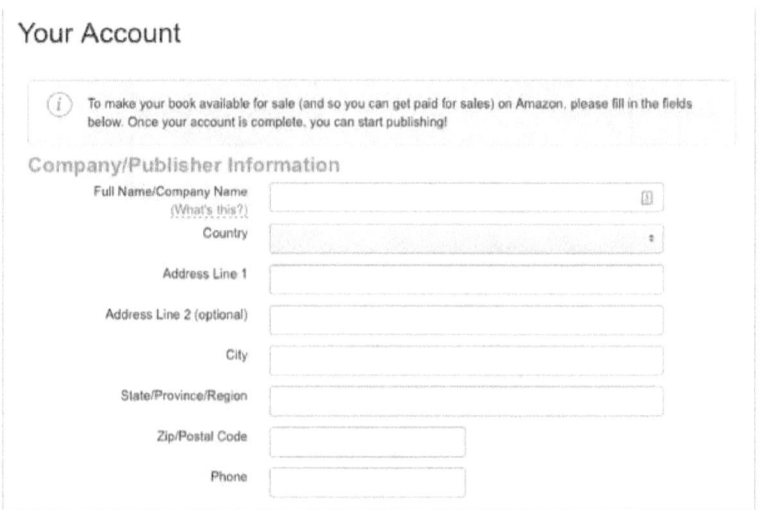

You will need to enter your financial information including social security number and bank account. If you refuse to tak ethis step, you can not open an account to publish books. There is a useful Tax Interview Guide on the right hand side of the box.

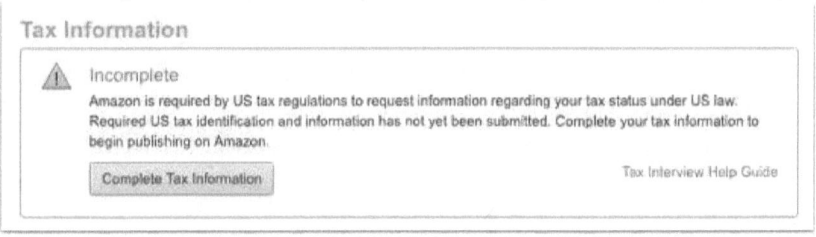

Once completed it will take a day or two for Amazon to verify your information. You will be paid monthly if your sales meet a certain minimum and at the end of the year, you'll receive a 1099 tax statement that you will file with your income tax return. You'll be paid the gross amount of royalties each month. Set at least 30% aside for your taxes.

Review the taxpayer identification form to ensure the accuracy of your previous inputs. If any fields are not correct, please go back to the relevant screen and update your information.

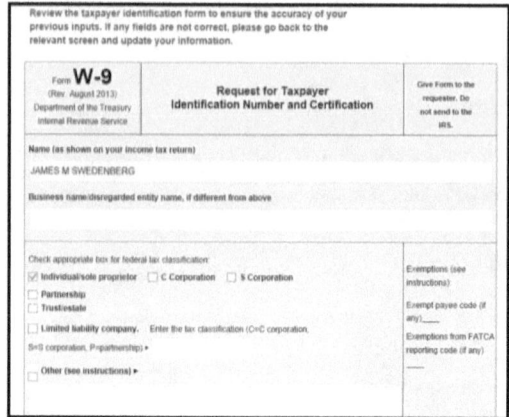

Form **W-9** (Rev. August 2013) Department of the Treasury Internal Revenue Service	**Request for Taxpayer Identification Number and Certification**	Give Form to the requester. Do not send to the IRS.

Name (as shown on your income tax return)

JAMES M SWEDENBERG

Business name/disregarded entity name, if different from above

Check appropriate box for federal tax classification:

☑ Individual/sole proprietor ☐ C Corporation ☐ S Corporation

☐ Partnership
☐ Trust/estate

☐ Limited liability company. Enter the tax classification (C=C corporation, S=S corporation, P=partnership) ▶

☐ Other (see instructions) ▶

Exemptions (see instructions)

Exempt payee code (if any)____

Exemptions from FATCA reporting code (if any)
____

Address (number, street, and apt. or suite no.)

City, state, country and ZIP code

Requester's name and address (optional)

List account number(s) here (optional)

Part I   Taxpayer Identification Number (TIN)

Enter your TIN in the appropriate box. The TIN provided must match the name given on the "Name" line to avoid backup withholding. For individuals, this is your social security number (SSN). However, for a resident alien, sole proprietor, or disregarded entity, see the Part I instructions on page 3. For other entities, it is your employer identification number (EIN). If you do not have a number, see How to get a TIN on page 3.

Note. If the account is in more than one name, see the chart on page 4 for guidelines on whose number to enter.

Social security number

Employer identification number

Consent to electronic 1099 form

In order for Amazon to provide an electronic version of your tax information reporting Form 1099, the IRS requires that we obtain your consent. If you do not provide consent for electronic delivery of your tax information reporting statements, you may still use the U.S. tax interview process to complete your IRS W-9 or W-8 form. However, at the end of the calendar year, we will mail your completed tax information reporting statements for your records.

If you provide consent for electronic delivery of your tax information reporting statements, you may revoke this consent at any time by retaking the tax information interview.

Note: At this time, not all Amazon businesses have enabled the electronic delivery of Form 1099. You may still receive a paper form from these businesses until the electronic delivery has been enabled.

Electronic 1099 form   ○ I consent to electronic receipt of my information reporting documentation
○ No, mail the documents to me

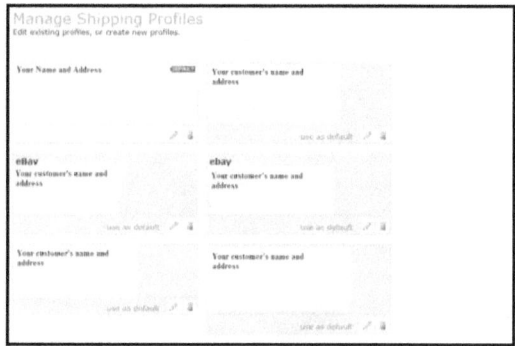

What is Expanded Distribution?

Royalty Date	Title	Royalty Type	Transaction Type	Units Sold
2019-03-27	Study Guide for the US Citizen	60%	Standard - Paperback	1
2019-03-22	Study Guide for the US Citizen	40%	Expanded Distribution Channels	60

Expanded Distribution allows you to sell across the worldwide market including retailers, bookstores, libraries, academic institutions, and distributors within the United States.

For more information visit:
https://kdp.amazon.com/en_US/help/topic/GQTT4W3T5AYK7L45

MS Word Tips
I don't know what you know or don't know.
Use Ctrl Z to reverse changes you don't like
Use Ctrl F to find words or series of words like Chapter
Use Find and Replace to speed up editing
If you make a specific edit, do them all at once, otherwise you might forget some.
Take one of the many free online courses for MS Word at
http://alison.com/courses/Microsoft-Word-2010

Open an Amazon Account

Follow the directions to build your Author's page. Go to Amazon.com, search for Mike Swedenberg in the Books category and open my Authors page.

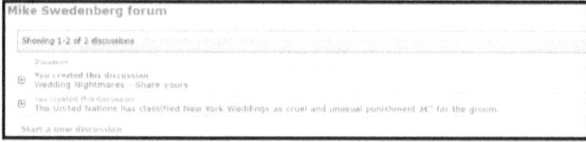

Class Three

Preparing Your Details

Three key compotes critical to your success, besides writing a great book, is the information you provide for prospective customers. They are the book's description, your biography (Bio) and the tags (metadata).

Book Description

The book description will tell potential customers that your book is all about. The best resource to learn how to write a killer description that is cutting edge is on Amazon.com's Best Seller List.

Select the Books Department and click on Best Sellers

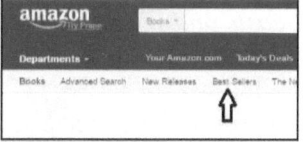

These are top three best sellers

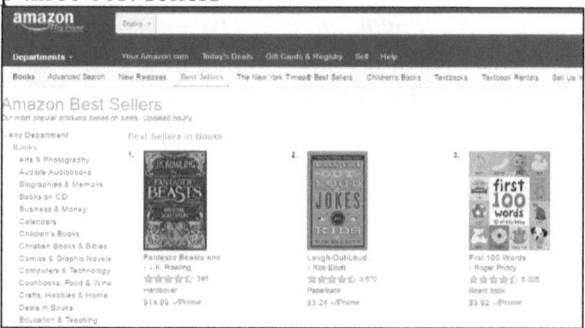

Click on the first book, which is always the number one best seller to reveal the details.

21

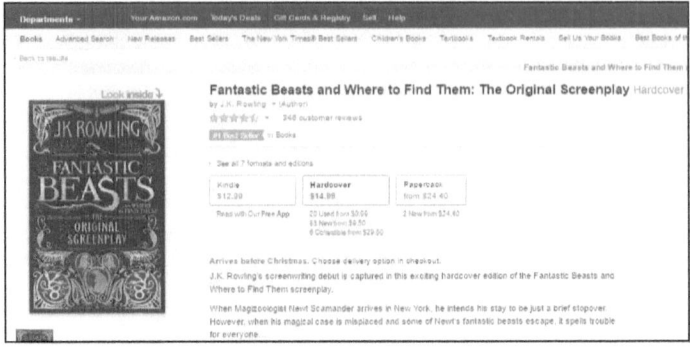

Scroll down to the description in italics. In this case, it starts with an announcement of Rowling's newest book. Professional, experienced copywriters create them, and you will learn a great deal by studying them.

J.K. Rowling's screenwriting debut is captured in this exciting hardcover edition of the Fantastic Beasts and Where to Find Them screenplay. (21 words)

The next paragraph is 37 words and a concise summary of the book.

When Magizoologist Newt Scamander arrives in New York, he intends his stay to be just a brief stopover. However, when his magical case is misplaced and some of Newt's fantastic beasts escape, it spells trouble for everyone...

Paragraph three mentions the title and author again reminding the reader of Rowling's success. It includes a line about the compelling characters and the adventure that awaits you.

Fantastic Beasts and Where to Find Them marks the screenwriting debut of J.K. Rowling, author of the beloved and internationally bestselling Harry Potter books. Featuring a cast of remarkable characters, this is epic, adventure-packed storytelling at its very best. (39 words)

The final paragraph has a <u>call to action</u> urging customers to buy a copy but in a non-aggressive manner. Instead of saying, go out and buy this book today, this editor used a subtle call to action.
Whether an existing fan or new to the wizarding world, this is a perfect addition to any reader's bookshelf. (19 words)

Why is this a valuable tool for you? A professional copywriter at Arthur A. Levine Books, an imprint of Scholastic Inc., wrote the book's description. The copywriter thought out every sentence, and even considered the number of words, 116 in this case. Note that there is no spoiler or book outline. Just enough information to entice the customer to buy.

Your assignment is to use this as a model for your book description. No, you're not J.K. Rowling, and you don't have her successful track record. However, there are things unique about you and your book.

Keep it under 140 words. Talk about the adventure or information you have to share. Use the same words and sentence structure found here. If it doesn't fit your book because you wrote a tour book of Italy or a Cajun Cookbook or a memoir of your time fighting in the Middle East, find a published book in your genre by a major book publisher and use one of those for a guide. By now you know what to look for and how it should be adapted.

How Pros write descriptions in other media.

Regardless if it's for a book, TV show or movie a well-written description is essential. Read these created by professional copywriters and see how they create interest in a program in 30 words or less.

"Conviction," ABC. A lawyer and former first daughter (Hayley Atwell) takes a job with the New York district attorney's office to avoid jail time for drugs and political damage for her mother's Senate campaign. (30 words)

"Notorious," ABC. A provocative look at the sexy and dangerous interplay of criminal law and the media. (12 words)

"Imaginary Mary," ABC. Jenna Elfman plays a fiercely independent career woman whose life is turned upside down when she meets the love of her life — a divorced father with three kids. (26 words)

"Downward Dog," ABC. Based on the web series, the comedy looks at the life of a struggling millennial (Allison Tolman) from the perspective of her philosophical dog, Martin. (26 words)

The Bio

http://authoritypublishing.com/book-marketing/how-to-write-a-dazzling-author-bio/

Examples of Effective Author Bios.

Patrick Schwerdtfeger Bio
Patrick Schwerdtfeger is a leading authority on global business trends including 'big data', self-employment and the social media revolution. He's the author of the award-winning book, Marketing Shortcuts for the Self-Employed (2011, Wiley) and a regular speaker for Bloomberg TV. Patrick has spoken about global mega trends, big data and the social media revolution at conferences and business events around the world.

Patrick A. Davey Bio
PATRICK A. DAVY graduated from the State University of New York College at Oswego with a BA degree in English Writing Arts. In addition, he studied creative writing at The Writers Group and Institute for Children's Literature in Connecticut. He lives on Long Island, New York with his family.

http://blog.hubspot.com/marketing/how-to-write-a-bio

My Bio written by a friend.
Mike Swedenberg has been publishing books for over ten years. He provides copywriting, coaching and teaches continuing education classes at Community Colleges on Long Island.

His educational background in business, sales, creative writing, and marketing has given him a broad base from which to approach many topics.

His writing skills are confirmed independently on Amazon.com He especially enjoys producing study guides and self-help books.
Sam Chinkes
Las Vegas, NV.

Now write your Bio thinking about your life achievements that directly relate to your expertise in writing your book. Write it in third person as if an Editor or someone who knows you well wrote it. It's how it's done. Write down everything you think of then cut it to 140 words.

Copyright Infringement

**I'm not an attorney and cannot offer legal advice.
Consult with a lawyer specializing in copyright law.**

Copyright Guidelines
The KDP Terms and Conditions require that "you hold the publishing rights to any content you upload for sale... Please do not upload or attempt to upload any material for which you do not have rights. The KDP Terms and Conditions allow us to reject or remove content from KDP and the Kindle Store. If you are unsure if you own the rights to the materials you wish to submit through KDP, please consult an attorney. While we do not require a copyright page, many publishers choose to include one. If you would like your book to have a copyright page, you must incorporate it into your content file. Please refer to our Copyright Guidelines for further details." - KDP

Reporting violations
Amazon respects the intellectual property of others. If you believe that your work has been copied in a way that constitutes copyright infringement, please follow the notice and procedure for the Amazon site where you identified the infringement.

To learn more about Copyrights, you may find it helpful to visit the United States Copyright Office at http://www.copyright.gov

Everything you publish must belong to you. If you download a photo from the internet, make sure you have paid for the rights to do so and retain the receipt. If you can't afford it, use your cell phone camera and take a similar photo. You can use it because you own it.

A woman I know pulled an image off of the internet and posted it on her company webpage. She did not pay for it, nor get permission from the owner of the photo. She didn't consider the legal ramifications. A month later she received a letter from the owner's lawyer demanding a payment of $4,000 for unauthorized use. Her attorney said to take the photo down and pay the owner the money. An expensive lesson in copyright law. Regardless if you're creating a book or webpage, don't take stupid chances. Remember, as a self-publisher, you're all on your own, and an attorney could charge you $350 an hour to defend you.

Don't use someone's face in a crowd unless you have their written permission. And for crying out loud never photograph someone's children even if you have the parent's permission. It could come back to haunt you.

Take a photo of an adult you know with their face obscured or cropped off above the mouth or from behind. You can find examples of this on the net. Study the best-selling books in your genre on Amazon by the big 5 publishers and see how they do it.

If you quote someone, make sure you give them credit and always cite your sources as I did above with http://www.copyright.gov.

Offensive Material

You may not be able to quote the definition of offensive material, but you know it when you see it. Amazon will not allow you to use, photos or videos of crime-scene, cruelty to animals, and extremely disturbing materials. Amazon reserves the right to determine the appropriateness of items sold on its site. Although you won't be posting videos in a print book, you could link to them in an eBook.

Be aware of cultural differences and sensitivities. Some materials may be acceptable in one country, but unacceptable in another. Please keep in mind our global community of customers."

Rights of Publicity

You may not use celebrity images and/or celebrity names for commercial purposes without permission of the celebrity or their agent. This means slapping Bill Gates photo on the cover of your high-tech mystery novel will land you in legal trouble and maybe court.

Using a product image on the cover that puts the product in a negative light could bring more legal grief.

Who Owns Your Work?

You retain ownership of your book contents, title, and cover design.

KDP owns the rights to their templates, and other tools used to publish your books.

Your Book is Published As Is.

KDP does not edit or modify the contents of your book; however, certain modifications may occur caused by file conversions. KDP does not guarantee accurate preservation of the original work's formatting. No one at KDP edits your book before it's published.

You're buk will bee published regardless of spulling, gramar and punctuation,,, errors!?:

Pricing Your Book

Oddly enough there are formulas and guidelines to pricing an eBook but not for print. I offer these suggestions.

1.)   Don't get greedy. Pricing your book far above the competition in your genre will kill off sales.

2.)   Check the top 20 selling books in your genre to determine what price range is driving sales. Too low of a price and readers will think your book has no value. Too high and you will just lose sales. In the example of my study guides for English and Spanish, I'm priced at $9.95 while my competitors are at $7.95. I'm consistently in the top 10 for sales. A competitor at $19.95 is in 85th place. He/she will make more per sale but have fewer sales. You can always go down in price but not up.

3.)   The big 5 publishers will always charge more. This gives you an advantage.

4.)   Experiment with the pricing each month until you find a sweet spot that works best for you.

5.)   KDP will tell you the minimum price you can set. Usually, that means you get no royalties for expanded distribution. Those are resellers who can buy in bulk at a discount. My resellers often buy 100 copies at a time to fill orders.

6.) Some people will offer copies of your book at ridiculously high prices. There is always someone out there who will pay $309 for one copy of my Study Guide rather than buy it from me for $9.95. I know it makes no sense but check for yourself. Go to my English Spanish Study Guide and click on Used copies. You'll get a pop-up window with all offers. In this case, click on the link for 8 used from $13.61. (This may change day to day.)

Here is the pop up with the choices for used books starting at $13.61 to $309 as opposed to a new copy for $9.95. I doubt these are actually used copies due to the nature of it being a study guide.

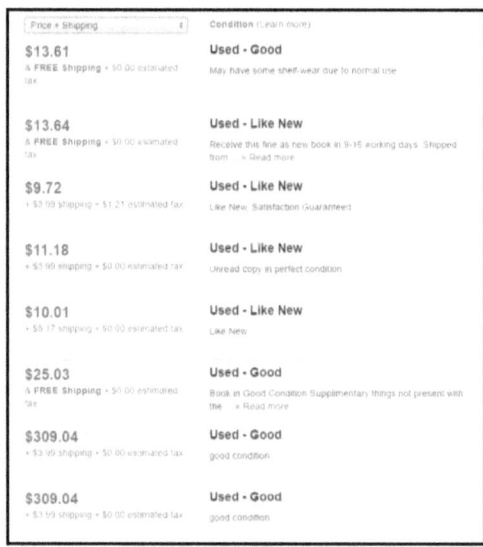

What are Tags?

A keyword (Metadata) attached to information, image, file or your book used to help readers find specific things on the internet. You choose the tags for your book by trial and error on Amazon.com to see what books you find. Don't use tags that repeat your title or description. They are already included. To do so is repetitious and limits other tags that would help bring your book to the top search results. Tags for the Smashwords Style Guide. Try them out for yourself.

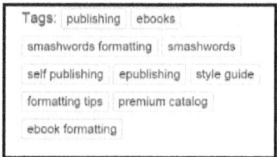

Google search for tag "eBooks"

Class Four - PRINT

Downloading and Using a KDP Formatted Template

You can download the book templates directly from KDP once you start to publish your book, but I suggest you find one before you start the publishing process.

Google: KDP formatting templates

The first search result should look like this, but you may have to scroll down to find it.

To find your template, click **Download**, open the ZIP folder, choose your language and trim size.

Download (Blank templates)

Download (Templates with sample content)

The most common trim size for paperbacks in the U.S. is 6" x 9" It is the best size to use for novels and non-fiction because it will fit on a standard book rack in a retail store.

For a children's illustrated book or a cookbook, find books similar to yours and see what size traditional publishing houses use. They have the best handle on marketing requirements. Remember the larger the book, the higher the postage rate and shipping material.

Visit your local bookstore or bn.com (Barnes & Nobel) and click on best sellers. Scroll to the bottom where they will list the product dimensions.

Where the Crawdads Sing – Hardcover by Delia Owens
Product dimensions: 6.10(w) x 9.10(h) x 1.30(d)

Amazon.com Books also list the size of paperbacks.

Supermarket – Paperback by Bobby Hall
Product Dimensions: 8 x 5 x 8 inches

The Process

To begin, open your KDP account Member Dashboard

https://kdp.amazon.com/en_US/bookshelf and click on "+ Paperback."

Create a New Title

Kindle eBook

Paperback

Book Content: You can upload a manuscript, or use our free creation tools to create children's books, educational content, comics, and manga. Get started with Kindle content creation tools.

Book Cover: You can use our online Cover Creator, or upload a cover of your own. Creating a great cover.

Description, Keywords and Categories: Tell readers about your book and help them find it on Amazon.

ISBN: Get a free ISBN to publish your paperback. Kindle eBooks don't need one. More about ISBNs.

See all Getting Started tips ›

The most important task is to prepare your book for uploading in the proper format. To get this correct template go to:

https://kdp.amazon.com/en_US/help/topic/G201834230

Or do an Internet search for the term: KDP print word templates

Either Google.com or DuckDuckGo.com will take you to the link.

There is a three-minute video on the page that will walk you through the steps.

In Step 1, you can download either a blank template (experienced level) or Templates with sample content. (novice level) I recommend you choose the one with sample content for your first book. The templates are easy to use but can be a bit quirky if you modify the default settings. Even with 25 titles published, I still use the Template with sample content because it's easier and faster.

Most of my writers had completed their books or were mostly done. In the four years with over 100 class attendees, not one had their book in the proper format. This required the process of cutting and pasting their book into the correct template. Ideally, you want to start writing in the template from the beginning. Save the link and download the template for your second book. It will save you hours of work.

Fill in the Title, select paperback, and the Guided tour. Make sure the title on this page matches the one on your book file exactly.

These templates include sample content to guide you, including front matter, chapters, headers, page numbers, etc. Additional tips. 6 x 9 is the fifth template on the list. Non-formatted templates are for advanced publishers who don't need the guidelines.

After you download the file, save a copy as a backup. Do a Save As naming it with your book title. Use this new copy for your book.

For those who don't know the difference, choosing "Save As..." brings up a prompt to save your work as a file with a different name. You might choose to save a document called "My book title" and do a Save As "My Book Title Revision A." Another Save As could be "My Book Title Revision B." This way, you can save your file at different stages and keep multiple versions on your hard drive.

Here is the 6 x 9 template for your book. When you open the Save As file it will appear like this:

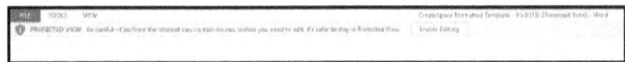

Click on Enable Editing.

You will see where the Title and your name goes. Type over the words Book Title and Author Name

The next page holds your copyright information. Although this is all that is required, I add an in-depth copyright page as seen in the front of this book. The text is below.

You may copy this and insert your name and contact information. By adding my publisher's email address, my readers can contact me. I've heard from distributors who wanted to carry my Study Guides.

I will add the ISBN numbers before I convert to a PDF and upload the file. It is one of the first steps when publishing on KDP. Once generated, cut and past the numbers on your book file.

The third page contains your dedication. Don't be thrown off by the words "Insert dedication text here." That is a placeholder letting you know where the text goes. Just type over it.

DEDICATION

Insert dedication text here. Insert dedication text here. Insert dedication text here. Insert dedication text here. Insert dedication text here. Insert dedication text here. Insert dedication text here. Insert dedication text here. Insert dedication text here. Insert dedication text here.

Mine:

DEDICATION

To my fellow writers who made the effort
and published their books.

The forth page is supposed to be blank. Don't delete it or add any text.

Page five has a sample Table of Contents. Don't try to make any changes. There is an automatic process that simplifies this, but it's one of the last things you do.

CONTENTS

The sixth page is blank as well. Don't add anything there.

The seventh page is marked in the footer. It has your Acknowledgements. It too has a placeholder, "Insert acknowledgments text here."

ACKNOWLEDGMENTS

Insert acknowledgments text here. Insert acknowledgments text here. Insert acknowledgments text here. Insert acknowledgments text here. Insert acknowledgments text here. Insert acknowledgments text here. Insert acknowledgments text here. Insert acknowledgments text here. Insert acknowledgments text here. Insert acknowledgments text here.

I replaced the Dedication with a Forward. It's optional.

Forward

The following is my 10-hour lesson plan
presented to Writers at
Nassau Community College, Garden City NY
and other Continuing Education Institutions.

Parts of my presentation involve classroom participation and reviews of author biographies and their book descriptions. We also experiment with searching tags, discussion of bestseller book covers and demonstrations of uploading books to publish. I have tried to recreate those in this book. If you have a question or a problem, you may email me at mike@swedenberg.com, and I will attempt to help you. No charge of course.

Best of luck and keep writing,

Mike Swedenberg

Page eight is blank.

Page Nine is where you place Chapter One. If you have already started your book in another document, you can cut and paste your book here. For best results do one chapter at a time. If you haven't begun your book, this is where you start writing. Just follow the template chapter by chapter. To make the Table of Contents automatic.

|1 CHAPTER NAME

Insert chapter one text here. Insert chapter one text here. Insert chapter one text here. Insert chapter one text here. Insert chapter one text here. Insert chapter one text here. Insert chapter one text here. Insert chapter one text here. Insert chapter one text here. Insert chapter one text here.
Insert chapter one text here. Insert chapter one text here. Insert chapter one text here. Insert chapter one text here.
Insert chapter one text here. Insert chapter one text here. Insert chapter one text here. Insert chapter one text here. Insert chapter one text here. Insert chapter one text here. Insert chapter one text here. Insert chapter one text here.
Insert chapter one text here. Insert chapter one text here. Insert chapter one text here.
Insert chapter one text here. Insert chapter one text here. Insert chapter one text here. Insert chapter one text here. Insert chapter one text here. Insert chapter one text here. Insert chapter one text here. Insert chapter one text here. Insert chapter one text here.
Insert chapter one text here. Insert chapter one text here. Insert chapter one text here. Insert chapter one text here.
Insert chapter one text here. Insert chapter one text here. Insert chapter one text here. Insert chapter one text here. Insert chapter one text here. Insert chapter one text here. Insert chapter one text here. Insert chapter one text here.
Insert chapter one text here. Insert chapter one text here. Insert chapter one text here. Insert chapter one text here.
Insert chapter one text here. Insert chapter one text here. Insert chapter one text here. Insert chapter one text here. Insert chapter one text here. Insert chapter one text here. Insert chapter one text here.

1

Add the book title in the header by double clicking on the top of the page and entering it. Look at the top of this page and the one opposite to see what I mean.

BOOK TITLE

one text here. Insert chapter one text here. Insert chapter one text here.

AUTHOR NAME

Insert chapter one text here. Insert chapter one text here. Insert chapter one text here. Insert chapter one text here. Insert chapter one text here.

37

Using the Style Buttons
You should not start work on your original book until you are comfortable with these features.

In the upper left-hand corner of the Word Doc screen, click on File then Save As to create a working copy of your book with a different name like TEST. Use this Test doc to experiment on the guidelines below. If you make a mistake and can't correct it, then you can create a new TEST copy without causing any harm to your original book.

Styles are formatting options in Word under the Home tab. They control things like the Font, Size, Color, and positioning on the page. If you set this up when you start your book, everything will be consistent throughout and professional in appearance.

When you write or import your book, use one style, preferably Normal. These choices are found on the Home tab.

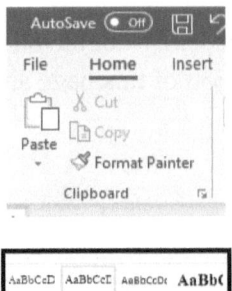

Right mouse click on the Normal button and select Modify to determine how the body of the text will appear.

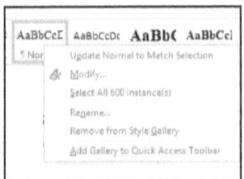

At the bottom of the popup you can select if you want that style to apply only to the book you are working on (choose this) or to every document in the future. (don't choose this unless you are working on similar projects and always want that style.) For this book I'm using Normal for Paragraphs, Times New Roman font in 11 point nothing is "Bold Italic" or "Underlined." I'll do those independently where appropriate.

The next row are the buttons for placing the text Flush Left, Centered, Flush Right and Justified. Always select the first option Flush Left. Other options control line spacing and indent. Leave those as they are. More options are available by clicking the Format button in the lower left-hand corner.

Once this is done, click on Select > Select All (in the upper right corner for Word 2013) This will highlight your entire book. Then click the Normal button and your entire book will be uniformly formatted. You never have to worry about it again.

Until you master these skills, KEEP IT SIMPLE. You may follow the same procedure using Headline 1. Modify it to your liking and use it for Chapter Headings. A detailed explanation can be found on Youtube.com or in the Alison.com courses I recommended earlier.

Recommendations:

The Body of your book should be Normal and Chapter Headings should be Heading 1 and Subheadings should be Headings 2. I'll show you what each does when you set up your Table of Contents.

Highlight your Chapter Title and Select Heading 1. (Forward)

Sub Headings (My Background) should be Heading 2 and there is the option of a Heading 3 (Published Works and Non Fiction)

Contents¶

Body of the text should be Flush left

Line spacing: Single or 1.5 but be consistent.

One space between paragraphs.

Page size: letter.

Margins: Use Word's standard print margins (Top and Bottom = 1", Left and Right = 1.25")

If you don't know what style a section is in, highlight it and look at the Styles tab at the top of the page. It will be framed in a grey border.

As with this book, non-fiction requires a Table of Content (TOC). It will not pass approval if one is missing. There is no need for a TOC in fiction although many writers put one in anyway.

You can use page breaks to control what text stays on a page, but I find them problematic. I don't use them except in print and even then, they can throw off the text on the next page.

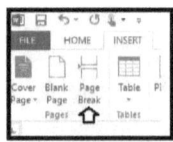

A page break will look like this when Show/Hide is activated. It is on the

Home tab and looks like a backward P

How to update a Table of Contents

When you make changes to the content of your books such as adding or removing chapters, headings on moving things around, the Table of Contents (TOC) will not automatically change. There is a simple way to update the TOC.

1.) Go to the TOC and right mouse click. The TOC will be highlighted.

2.) A pop will appear. Click on Update Field.

3.) A second pop up will appear. Choose update page numbers only, If you haven't changed any of the heading titles. As an example, you have made adjustments that moved Chapter 2 from page 15 to page 16, you only have to update the page number. If you have changed the name of the heading from My background to My education, eliminated it or added a new one, you need to update the entire table. Then press OK. Make sure to do this as a final step before you save to PDF to upload.

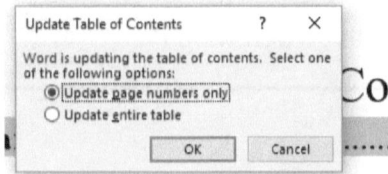

4.) If the heading in your book is in a bold font, it will appear bold in the TOC. If you don't like the mix of bold and regular fonts, after you update it, highlight the TOC and toggle the **B** button on the Home Page Font tab to make the TOC uniform.

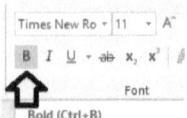

How to insert images, tables, and charts.

Using the "Insert Picture" feature

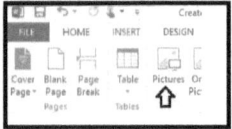

It is best to insert either JEPG or PING photographs. Charts, tables, and graphs can't be created in the Word document. If you need these for your eBook, you can create them on another document and save them as an image. Once done you can import from your computer or digital camera as you would a photograph. Set the resolution at 250 dpi. (dots per inch)

A discussion on changing the DPI on an image is found later in this chapter.

Viewing You Book's Layout

When you have completed your book and have all the sections filled in, there is an easy way to look at your book and the way it will appear in print. On the top of the word Document, click on the View tab.

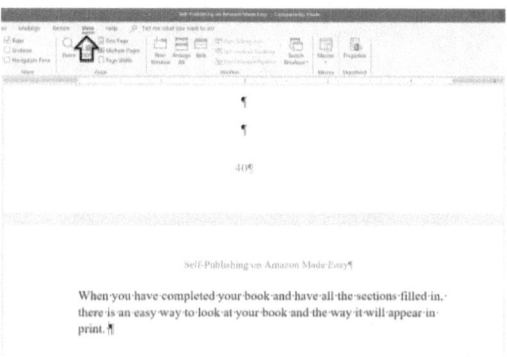

Click on Multiple Pages.

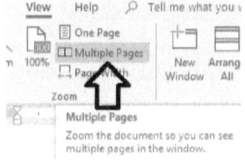

The view of your book on screen will increase to three pages across from one. This allows you to see any glaring issues with the way the text is lined up across the page and if there are any large gaps that don't belong. You want the top line of each page to be the same height on the page as the others. They don't have to be lined up across the bottom. If You need a better visual, look at any printed book you have. This is the time to make adjustments.

For an even smaller page view, Click on View as before, then on Zoom and select 75%

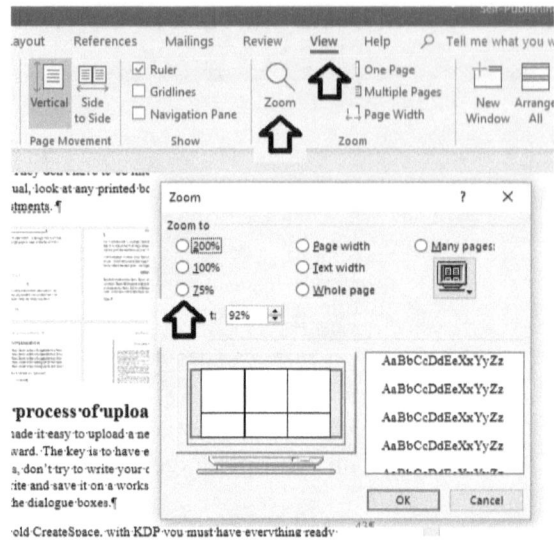

You will see 4 pages across the screen depending on your monitor size. Mine measures 27 inches diagonally. Or, enter the percent number you want in the small window below the 75% button. You can reverse this at any time by clicking on Zoom and choosing either the 100% or 200% view. None of these actions will alter the way your book is printed. When working on my book, I prefer the 200% view because it causes less eye strain.

Book Cover Design.

Study the professionally designed book covers found on the New York Times Best Seller List especially those from the big 5 publishers.
Amazon.com > Search in Books: New York Times Bestseller list for 2017

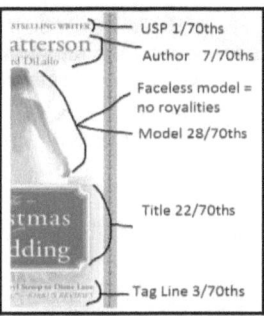

Note how the cover design is broken into segments. I used a printer's Pica ruler to divide the cover into 70 units. Lacking one, use a standard ruler and divide the page into 16ths of an inch. For this 8-inch high book, it would be 128 units. Study the proportions of the font size for the Author's name and the title.

Now study the Best Seller list for cover designs in your genre. Keep in mind what's good for a romantic novel isn't necessarily good for a non-fiction like a biography although good design elements prevail across the board.

This is a cover I created for a nonexistent book based on an actual cover design. It can be a well-written book, but the cover is a lead weight holding it down. It's a perfect example of a self-published author with no sense of design.

The cover design for *A Gentleman in Moscow* by Amor Towles is simple and elegant. The model is facing away eliminating any model release forms or royalties. If this is the design you think is good for your book, use it as a layout for yours. Use your imagination and make it your own.

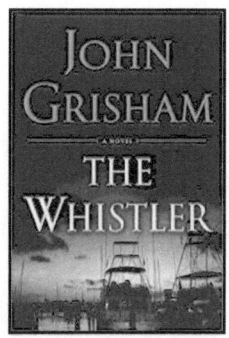

Here is a great cover design for John Grisham's *The Whistler*. I converted it to black and white to show the design elements. Using this as inspiration, I chose a photo I took last year in Naples Florida. I made up a title, *That Summer Day*, to create a book cover for a novel.

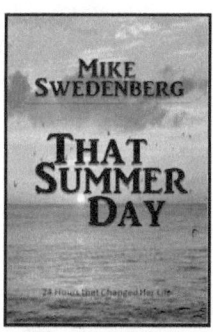

I spent nine minutes creating this cover in PowerPoint and it looks better in color. Given time, I could tighten up the design, but as a first draft you can see the elements of The *Whistler*. That is your objective.

How to Create a Cover PDF for your Book

Before the CreateSpace (CS) KDP merger, CS had a dynamic book cover temple program that helped writes create a first-rate book cover. As of this writing, KDP has not adopted that program. They do have templates you can use but they are limited to scope. To create a top-quality cover, you may need to hire a graphic designer to prepare the cover for you, if you don't have the software or skills to make your own. You will need to give them the template (below), your page count and photographs you want for the cover and author's photo.

The spine width of your book

The number of pages in your book determines the width of the spine. Bully Boss is 5.25" x 8" (13.335 x 20.32 cm) Black & White on white paper and 230 pages in length. That makes the spine 9/16" wide. You need to take this into account when you design your book cover. Most of my study guides are 100 pages long and are too thin to have any text on the spine. I used the CS cover template to create this for my novel. I supplied the images for the cover and author pic. I bought the rights to the cover image. I used a photo I took at the beach as my original publisher's logo.

There will always be some variation when books are bound. To compensate, you should leave 0.0625" variance on both sides of the fold lines for your cover. For a 1" spine, your text should be no wider than 0.875". KDP suggests that if your book is less than 130 pages you should have a blank spine. Keep in mind that online customers will not see your spine when shopping.

Exact formatting requirements from the KDP website:

For black and white-interior books

White paper: multiply page count by 0.002252
Cream paper: multiply page count by 0.0025

Example of spine width calculation for a 60-page black and white book printed on white paper: 60 x 0.002252 = 0.135"

For color-interior books
Multiply page count by 0.002347

Example of spine width calculation for a 60-page color book:
60 x 0.002347 = 0.141"

How to set up your document

Your cover must be a single PDF that includes the back cover, spine, and front cover as one image.

You can submit your cover on any size page as long as the printable area is:

- Measured exactly to your book's trim size, spine width, and .125" bleed

- Centered horizontally and vertically

Minimum Cover Width: Bleed + Back Cover Trim Size + Spine Width + Front Cover Trim Size + Bleed

Example calculation at 6" x 9" cover with 60 B&W pages on white paper: 0.125" + 6" + 0.135" + 6" + .125" = 12.385"

Minimum Cover Height: Bleed + Book Height Trim Size + Bleed

Example calculation: 6" x 9": 0.125" + 9" + .125" = 9.25"

Get a head start with one of KDP's cover templates

KDP templates make it easier for you to create print-ready files in Adobe Photoshop®, Adobe InDesign®, or any software that will allow you to open a .png or PDF file and save a PDF file. These templates contain the proper dimensions, layout, and bleed for the trim size and page count you select.

Look for this link: Download Cover Templates

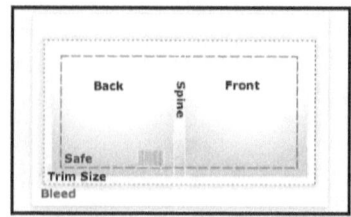

The Safe Zone
Since the trimming process is not exact, the text and images must be at least .125" inside the trim lines.

The Title and Author's Name
Your book's title and Author's name must match exactly to what you entered during the title setup. If you entered the title *The Good Times Ended* on the set up you can't change the cover title to *The Good Times Have Ended* or some other variation. KDP will require you to correct it further delaying the launch date of your book. The Author's name must appear on the interior file (your book) along with the title.

KDP does not required that the title name appear on the front cover if it is on the spine. However unless you have a compelling reason to omit the title from the cover, you should place it there. If your book does not have at least 101 pages, you can't put any text on the spine.

Your Images
Images may be CMYK, a four-color process used in color printing. It refers to the four inks used Cyan, Magenta, Yellow and Key, which is a printers' symbol for the color Black.

Images may also be RGB, which represents the three primary colors Red, Green and Blue. When mixed together they produce the secondary colors. When the press lays yellow ink on the cover and then adds blue on top of it, the result will be green. Red + Blue = Green

Google: "CMYK Images" and "RGB Images" without the quote marks for examples.

Size all images at 100%, flattened to one layer and placed in your document at a minimum resolution of 300 Dots per Inch. (DPI)

Dots Per Inch refers to the sharpness of the image. The more dots, the cleaner the image and the more it can be enlarged without the loss of sharpness.

See the illustration on the next page.

Open a photo from your computer, right mouse click on it and choose Properties at the bottom of the list. A new window will open revealing the details of the photo. You may have to click on the Details tab. This shows you the DPI of my image is 72 DPI which is fine for certain uses but not for printing.

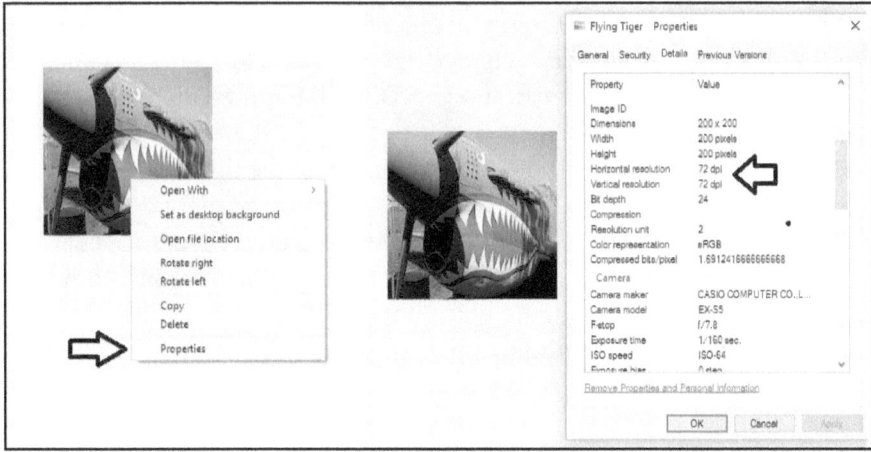

When I enlarged a section of the 72 DPI photo by 500%, you can see the poor quality. We call the ragged texture Pixilation. It causes the dots or squares to be visible. Many free apps are available to increase the DPI of your images. Keep in mind that the higher the DPI the smaller the image will be. KDP will alert you of all low-quality images; however they don't require you to fix them.

The Barcode

When your files go through the review process, The KDP system will place your ISBN barcode in a 2" by 1.2" white box in the lower right-hand corner of your book's back cover. The standard trim size templates will show you the exact barcode placement.

Images or text in the barcode location will be covered when the book is printed. Make sure no important elements appear where the barcode will be placed.

If you choose to provide and place your own barcode, be sure it is a high-resolution image. The barcode can be located on the back or front cover of your book, at a recommended size of 2" wide by 1.2" tall. You are welcome to add an additional UPC barcode for distribution purposes if applicable.

Prepare for Printing

1. The printable area of your document must be the right size, including bleed.

2. Make sure the printable area is centered within your document.

3. Make sure all live elements are inside the safe zone.

4. Export your file as a print-ready PDF. Be sure to embed fonts.

5. The maximum accepted file size for your book cover is 40 MB.

6. Download the KDP Submission Specification in one document.

Key Print Terms
Spine: The part of the cover that wraps around the bound edge of the book.

Trim: Where the page will be cut.

Bleed: To print at or off the very edge of a page by design. Commonly used to accommodate images and illustrations.

Live Elements: The content within the viewable area (or safe zone) which is always seen. No essential elements are cut during the bookmaking process.

The process of uploading your print book

KDP has made it easy to upload a new title, and the steps are straightforward. The key is to have everything ready when you start. In other words, don't try to write your description and Bio when you upload. Write and save it on a worksheet for your book. Then you cut & paste into the dialogue boxes.

Unlike the old CreateSpace, with KDP you must have everything ready to upload to proceed through the publishing process. You are not allowed to start the process and save for later until you reach the bottom of the page.

Step 1: Log not your account on the Bookshelf tab that you have already set up and click on Paperback:

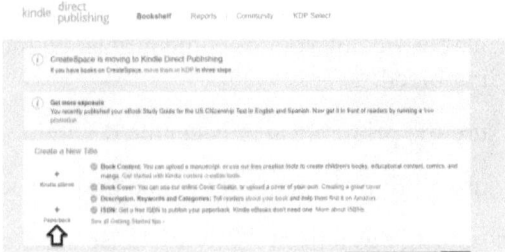

Step 2: This will open a new page where you can fill in the details of your book. The first three are Language, Book Title Subtitle and Series.

Once you have submitted the Title and Subtitle to get your ISBN, it can not be changed. Make sure this is the one you want to use.

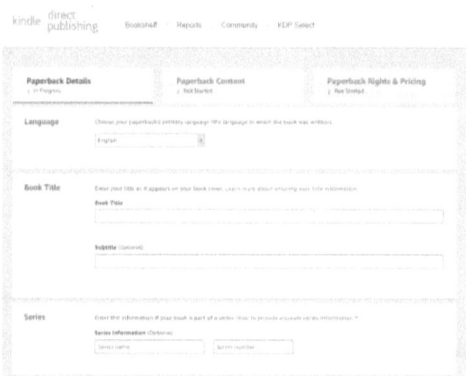

<u>Language:</u> Enter the primary one used in your book. There are no Bilingual options. That is why my English/Spanish study guide is listed as English. For me to classify it as Spanish, then the majority of the book and title would have to be in Spanish.

<u>Book Title:</u> Enter the title of your book. Again, once submitted it can not be changed even if you spot a typo later. The title and author name are linked automatically when you publish the Kindle version of the same book. For more detail click on the hyperlink: Learn more about entering your title information.

<u>Subtitle:</u> This is an option. The title of Joseph Conrad's novel is *The Secret Agent*. The Subtitle is *A Simple Tale*. The Title of Ford Madox Ford's novel is *The Good Soldier*. The subtitle is *A Tale of Passion*. Once the ISBN has been generated it can't be changed.

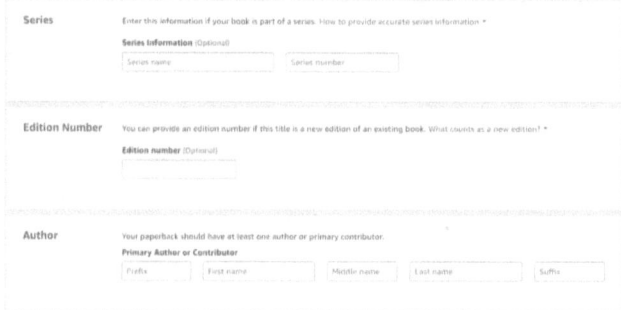

<u>Series:</u> The series name and volume number help group your books, and make it easier for your readers to find the next installment. An example

is the best selling *Longmire* series by Craig Johnson. Book 1 is *The Cold Dish*. Book 2 is *Death without Company* and the Third book is *Kindness Goes Unpublished*. More best selling series are *Lord of the Rings* by J. R. R. Tolkien and Harry Potter by J.K Rowling. Find them on Amazon Books and see how they are grouped and numbered. If yours is a stand alone book then leave series blank.

Edition Number: This refers to a version of your book. The first time you publish, enter 1 in the field for 1st Edition. You can't add the "st" in the field, just the number 1. If later, you make significant changes to the contents, you must republish on KDP with a new ISBN. You would enter 2 in the field to indicate it's the 2nd Edition. The rule is if you add more than 20% new contents for it to be a new edition. This means if you either add more content or make significant changes to existing content.

As an example, my *Study Guide for the US Immigration Test* was published in 2014 as the 1st Edition. I am up to the 10th edition for 2019, because I made significant changes with each year and general election. Minor changes, such as adding or removing a paragraph or two, and correcting typos do not require a new edition or ISBN.

Author: This is where you put your name or a pen name. If you co-authored the book, decide who gets top billing then click Add Another for the second contributor.

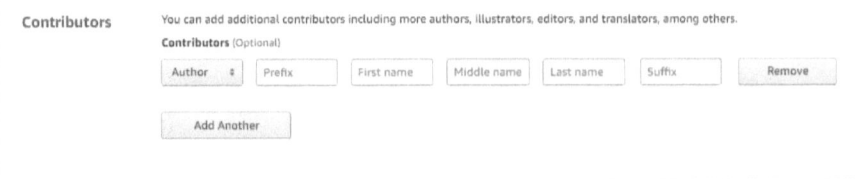

Contributors: A pull-down menu allows you to add an editor, illustrator or others who contributed. It is professional to give credit to those who helped make your book possible. If you did all of the work yourself, **do not** add your name in each category.

Always ask permission before you do add a contributor's name. Some may not want to be associated with your book. I once hired an editor to review one of my novels. She was happy to help me and take my money, but she only wanted to be associated with traditionally published works. I respected her wishes.

Description: People browsing for a book to read, need a well written, concise description to understand what your book is about. Take a look at any best seller on Amazon by a traditional publisher for examples of length and wording. Find one on your genre and use it as a model.

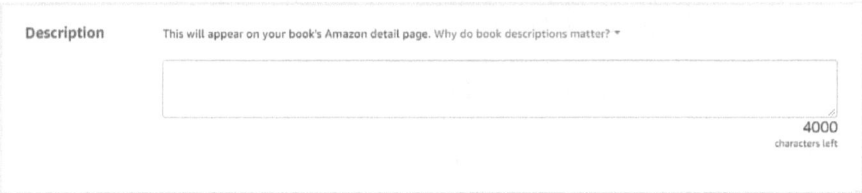

Publishing Rights: If you authored the book, you own the copyright. You can spend about $35 and register the book with the Copyright office, and many first time authors do thinking it will protect them 100%. I can not give legal advice, but I can say with all of my titles, I have never registered a book with the copyright office. I think it's a waste of time and money. Here is the government website: https://copyright.gov/

| Publishing Rights | ○ I own the copyright and I hold necessary publishing rights. What are publishing rights? ▾ |
| | ○ This is a public domain work What is a public domain work? ▾ |

The second option is for Public Domain work. It is important for you to understand what this is and to adhere to the rules.

The Public Domain is all of the creative works to which no exclusive intellectual property rights apply. Those rights may have expired, been forfeited, expressly waived, or may be inapplicable. You can publish material that is in the public domain but it has to be modified or enhanced with other material.

"The works of William Shakespeare and Beethoven, and most early silent films, are in the public domain either by virtue of their having been created before copyright existed, or by their copyright term having expired. Some works are not covered by copyright, and are therefore in the public domain—among them the formulae of Newtonian physics, cooking recipes, and all computer software created prior to 1974." - Wikipedia

Below is the link and a summary of the rules.

From the KDP website:
https://kdp.amazon.com/en_US/help/topic/G200743940

1. Publishing Public Domain Content

2. KDP allows the selling of content that is in the public domain.

3. You may need to provide proof that your content is in the public domain.

4. KDP may refuse public domain content that is already available through their program or other retail sites.

5. KDP won't publish undifferentiated versions of public domain titles if a free version is available in their store.

Differentiated works must one or more of these requirements:

Translated: Unique translations. *My Study Guide for the US Immigration Test in English and Spanish* has a unique translation because I hired someone whose native language is Spanish and speaks fluent English to put her unique spin on the translation.

Annotated: Unique annotations (additional content like study guides, literary critiques, detailed biographies, or historical context) My study guides contain legal advice from an Immigration attorney and the list of representatives from each state that one must know for the test. No other study guide offers these same features.

Illustrated: 10 or more unique illustrations relevant to the book. I do not have illustrations in my book, but it's not necessary because I have other unique features.

Visit the KDP website for compete rules.

Keywords: They help make your book discoverable and easier to find on Amazon. They must accurately portray your content and words readers may use in a search. You may not use words that misrepresent your book. Using "Harry Potter" as a keyword for your memoir because it would increase your book's ranking is a violation of KDPs terms, and you could get sanctioned. Some of the keywords I used for my study guide include USCIS, test, naturalization, and civics. I test different keywords by using Amazon's search window to see what results it would generate.

Keywords	Choose up to 7 keywords that describe your book. How do I choose keywords? ▾
	Your Keywords (Optional)

I tested "naturalization" as a keyword for my book, and it took me to the Amazon page with the Immigration study guides. As you can see, this is a strong keyword. It's not necessary to use words in your title, they are already included.

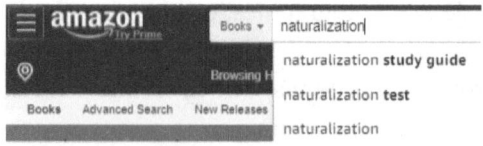

Categories: Choose the category for your book. At this point you should know which one to select. Under each category there are sub categories. As an example, click on the + sign next to Fiction when you are online.

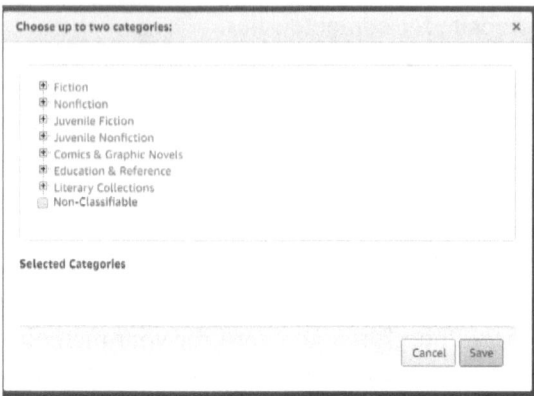

Another window will pop up with the subcategories. There could be as many as 50 from which to choose.

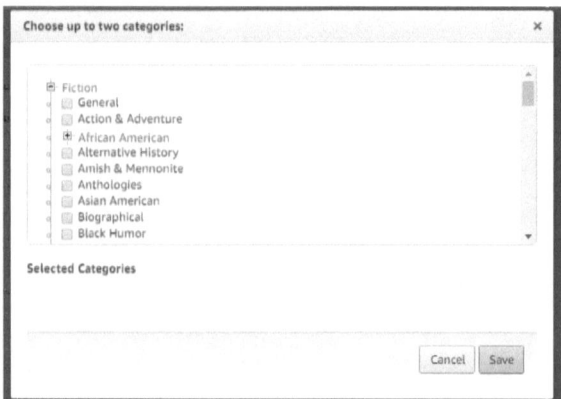

If you're not sure, find a similar book on Amazon and scroll down to show the categories they have used.

Delia Owens's paperback *Where the Crawdads Sing,* is listed in the

Fiction category and the subcategories of Coming of Age and Women's Friendship. If a third subcategory is listed, it's there because Amazon made the addition based on sales. You may select two.

#12 in **Coming of Age** Fiction (Books)

#28 in **Women's Friendship** Fiction

#38 in **Women's Domestic Life** Fiction

Intentionally selecting the wrong categories as a way to boost your sales is a violation of Amazon's user agreement and can result in your book being removed from sale and your account being closed.

Adult Content:

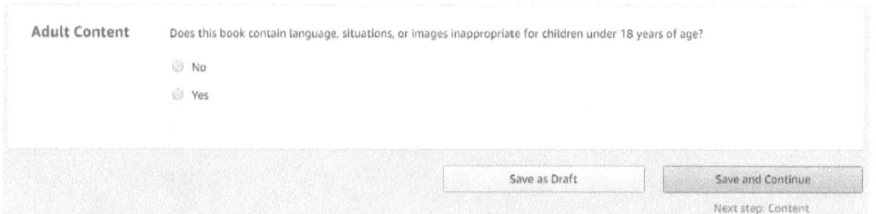

**I can't stress enough how important this step is to your sales. You may have authored the next great American novel, but if you select the wrong category it will be lost in the crowd.
Do your research beforehand.**

When you are done, click on SAVE and CONTINUE. Wait for the next page to load. If it doesn't load, it's because you left a required field blank. You'll see this warning at the top of the page.

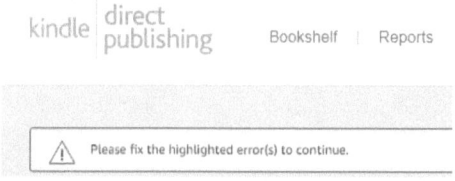

Scroll down and correct the error, then hit Save and Continue. In this example, I didn't add the Author's name. You can not proceed until it's completed. There may be more than one.

Page Two

You are now on Paperback Content. Step one is the ISBN.

KDP defines this as: "An ISBN, or International Standard Book Number, is a unique 10-digit number assigned to every published book. An ISBN identifies a title's binding, edition, and publisher. An EAN, or European Article Number, is a 13-digit number assigned to every book to provide a unique identifier for international distributors. The 10-digit ISBN is converted to a 13-digit EAN by adding a 978 prefix and changing the last digit. To publish a book, you can use either a free KDP ISBN or use your own valid ISBN (purchased directly from your ISBN agency)."

Here is the ISBN as displayed on the back of one of my books.

I use the free ISBN from KDP because it suits my needs. I do know other writers who buy their own from any number of services. Prices vary widely from $18 on up, and some services require you buy a block of ISBNs. You can find them with Google search: buy an ISBN number.

To determine what works best for you, Google search:
advantages of buying an ISBN number

This window gives you the option to publish immediately or at a later date.

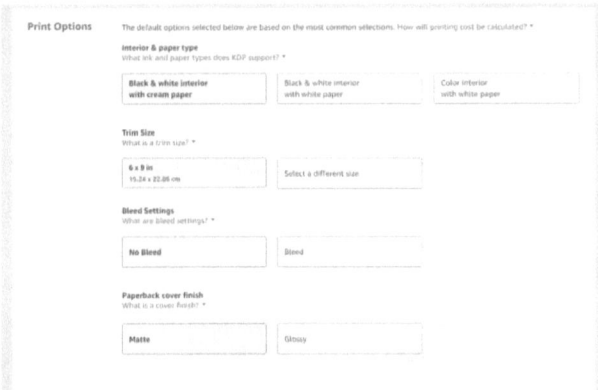

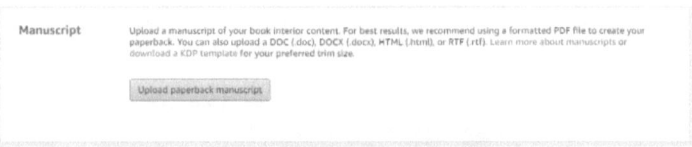

Once you have completed your book and saved it to a PDF, click on the Upload Paperback Manuscript button. It is best to upload a PDF because it locks in your formatting and nothing will change during the process. I used to upload the Word documents, but when I previewed the book, I found lines and images had been moved. To save your Word doc to a PDF, click on File > Save as type > Save As. You'll get a pop up with the choices. PDF is the seventh choice down. Always save your PDF to your desktop making it easy to find on your PC. If you must make more changes, delete the old PDF and replace it. To eliminate confusion, I will add a number to the end of the file name: Self-Publishing on Amazon Made Easy 1. If I make more edits, the new PDF will be saved as Self-Publishing on Amazon Made Easy 2 and so forth.

The next step is to use Cover Creator to build your own cover. It is a simple step by step process where you can use KDP's boiler plate designs and stock photos or upload your own high-resolution image. The best thing is you don't have to worry about placing the title, subtitle, or your name. It's already on the template. You can modify each, change the colors, fonts, and images until you get something you are happy with. Again, use the bestselling books on Amazon for ideas. The second option is to upload a PDF cover you have created using your own software or have paid a graphic artist to make for you.

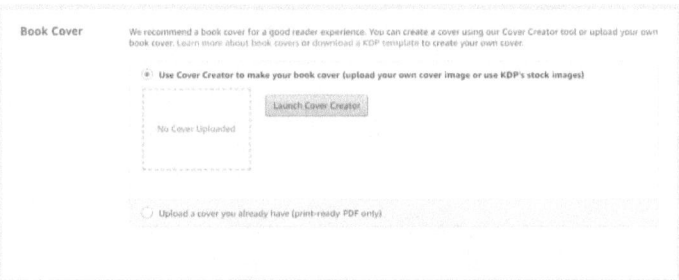

Click on Launch Cover creator and the program will open a new window.

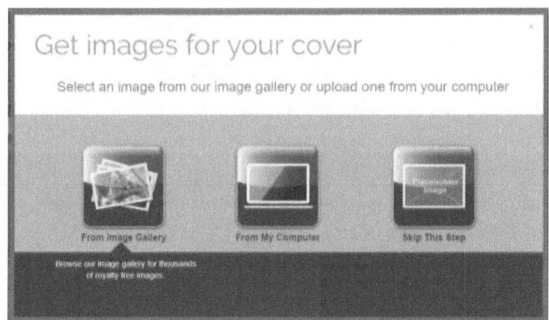

Select an image from KDP's gallery or upload your own. Don't be intimidated by using your own photo. If you have a good quality smartphone camera, a Point and Shoot or digital SLR you can take your own creation. To use your own, click on From My Computer and select the image you have saved.

Never use a photo you copied from the internet without permission. You can get sued. Especially since it's being used for commercial purposes.

From the Image Gallery, find a phot that best suits your cover. In this case I chose Animals, then Pets and finally a beagle. Click on Use this Image and you'll get a selection of cover designs.

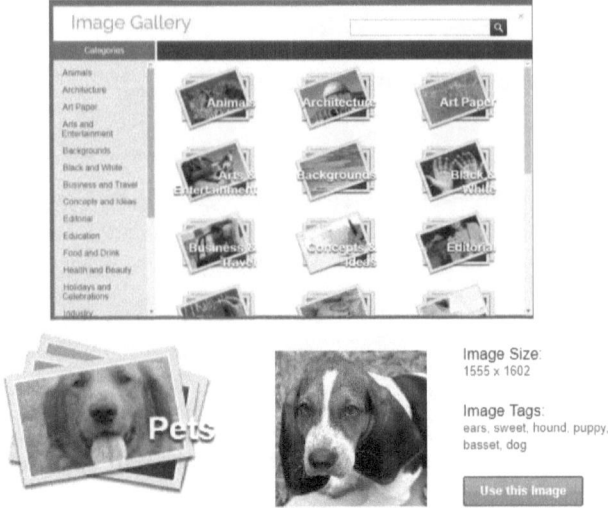

Now you have dozens of designs from which to choose. For this exercise, I used New Book as the title for demonstration purposes. Use the left and right arrows to select different layouts.

Once you have chosen your book cover, you will cut and past the text for the back cover. The text that is there is called Greek, it's just gibberish used as a filler to show you where you place your text. The back page can be the same information you used in the description. Remember a bookstore is different than online where customers usually don't see the back cover.

If you choose, upload a great photo of yourself. Check the best seller list to get ideas of what pose you should use. Make sure it's in focus, and straight. People like to see the author's face.

If the book is less than 100 pages, there will be no title on the spine.

The barcode area is left blank and will be added when the book is printed.

The next step is to preview your book online and approve it for publishing. Do so from front to back and look at each page. If there are mistakes, this is the time to fix them. Once published, any errors will be out there for people to buy. Even if you upload a new PDF, the old one will not be updated.

Click on Save and Continue.

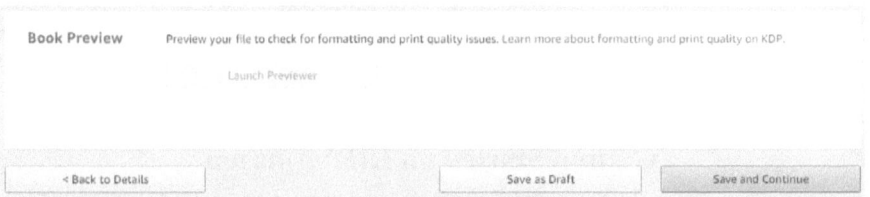

Class Five

Following is an overview of converting your print book to Kindle, something I urge you to do.

Screenshots used with permission. This book is in no way endorsed or sponsored by KDP, Amazon, or their affiliates. Brand names, logos and trademarks used herein are the property of their respective owners.

KDP.Amazon.com

Kindle Direct Publishing is a platform that allows Independent authors to self-publish their books in print as well as eBooks on Kindle.

While the publishing task takes less than 5 minutes, writing a quality book, formatting it properly, designing a book cover, writing your biography, book description and metadata tags is time consuming.

Some of the benefits of self-publishing with KDP.Amazon are:

1.) High royalties between 35 and 70%.

2.) Worldwide distribution in the US, Canada, Brazil, Mexico, Italy, Spain, UK, Germany, France, India, Japan, and Australia.

3.) You retain rights to your book, list price and have the option to make changes to the books content, cover design and key words whenever you want. You do not have this control in the traditional publishing world where someone else makes the decisions.

Getting Started on KDP.Amazon

Whenever you are unsure what each step requires or what it means, click on the (What's this r Why?) link for a popup window. It will reveal more information. I have done so for the following steps.

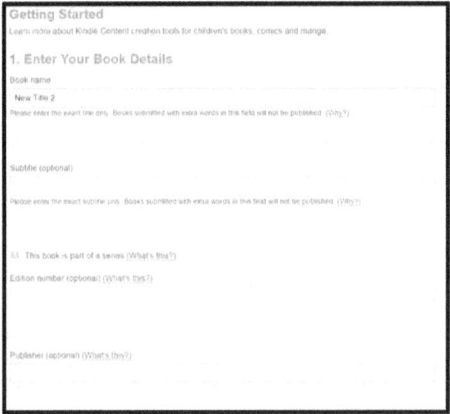

Edition number

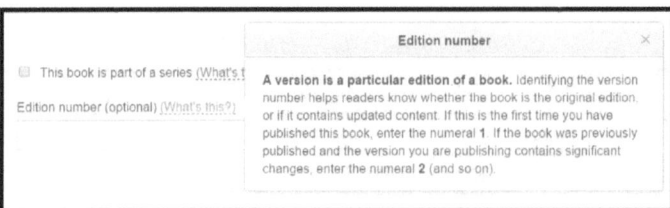

An Edition number is different from a Series number as you will see below discussed for Smashwords.

An edition number compromises all copies of a book printed at any time without substantial change.

In the world of POD you can upload a new file with minor changes or corrections. This does not affect the edition number. However if you make substantial changes in the book, add new chapters, eliminate others or provide up to date information, then you would change the edition number.

As an example, my first Study Guide for the US Immigration Test in English and Spanish published in 2010 was the 1st Edition. As I made minor changes, the edition number stayed the same. When we had the midterm elections, I updated the representatives' names and that made it the 2nd edition. The English/Spanish Study Guide for 2017 is now the 9th edition.

When you publish your novel, it will be a 1st edition. If you don't make major changes, the Edition number will never change.

Publisher

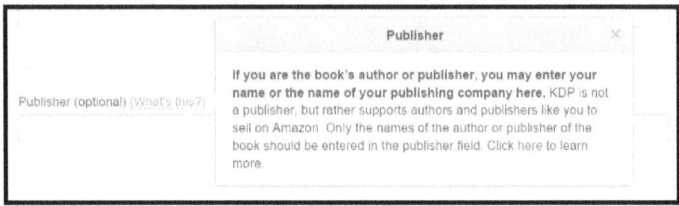

You are the publisher, not KDP.Amazon. If you wish you may enter your name here or a business name if you are incorporated. If you use a pen name for your book, you can use your real name as publisher if you choose. My publishing name is James M. Swedenberg while my pen name is Mike Swedenberg.

Amazon Series

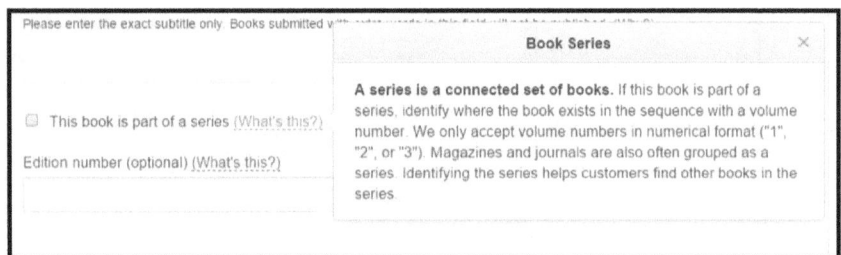

As a review, a Series is a group of books with the same Title and different subtitles like The Game of Thrones. In that series you'd find A Game of Thrones, A Clash of Kings, A Storm of Swords, A Feast for Crows, A Dance with Dragons. This makes it easier for the series fans to find George R. R. Martin's books.

The Series name for my self-publishing books is Get Published. The Series name for my US Citizenship books is Study Guides for the US Citizenship Test Translated and Annotated.

Description

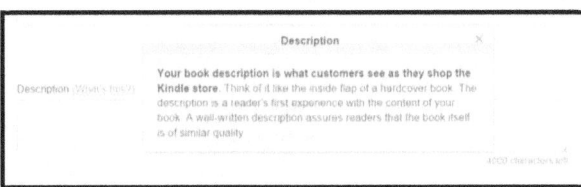

The description can entice the reader to learn more about your book and perhaps make a purchase or turn him/her off completely and move on. Here are some suggestions.

1. You're writing an Advertisement not a book summary. Authors are usually too emotionally invested in their books to write an objective description. Look at the descriptions on Amazon for the best-selling books in your genre. Use them as a blueprint for you own book.

2. Make the first sentence compelling enough to force them to read the rest of the description. Again, look at the professionally written descriptions.

3. Don't compare your book to a best seller as in: The Next Harry Potter. No one will believe you and you will appear desperate and amateurish.

4. If you've published other books that have sold well then including "By the Author of..." is a good thing to do. Mine is "A New York Wedding, by the author of Bully Boss."

5. Bullet points are great. They draw attention.

6. Some guidelines to consider. Amazon Bestsellers have descriptions that are about 150 in two paragraphs. As with your biography use third person. Keep it simple with short clear statements. Don't make your readers struggle with your description.

7. Add Contributors

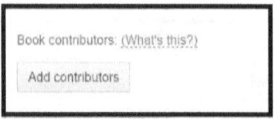

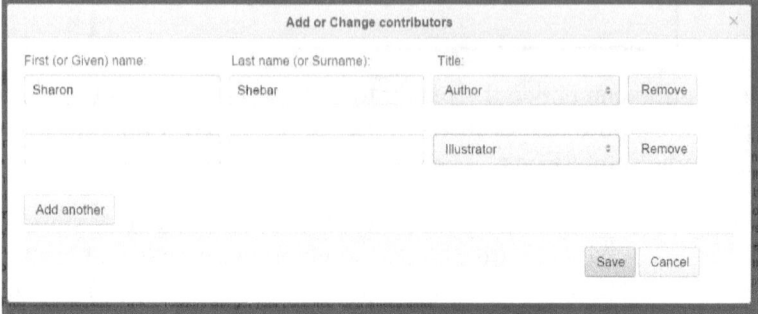

It's professional to give credit to others who helped bring your book to life. It's a simple process to add the editor, cover designer and or the photographer's name to the books description. They will not share in the royalties of your book unless you have made arrangements for their compensation. The royalty checks come to you and you are responsible to pay others. Since I paid my contributors up front, I keep all royalties. You should do the same.

Here is an example of how it appears on Amazon

A New York Wedding

by Mike Swedenberg (Author), Wendy Quirk (Designer)

Language, ISBN and Publishing Rights

The pull down menu allows you to select the language. Unfortunately it is restricted to only one. My bilingual study guides are all listed as English. If I were to select Spanish, Amazon would want the cover to be in Spanish as well. For my books this would not work.

ISBN (International Standard Book Number), as discussed earlier is an identifier for print books. eBooks and Print can't share the same ISBN. You would have to purchase an ISBN for your Kindle book. If you choose not to, then KDP.Amazon will provide you with a 10-digit ASIN (Amazon Standard Identification Number) at no charge.

The ASIN for the Kindle version of A New York Wedding is B00T4ZFT1M while the ISBN for the print version is ISBN-13: 978-1503007932. They can't be interchanged.

Target your book

Categories. Choose the right one and you can be the number one best seller. Choose the wrong one and the same book will languish in obscurity. Why? Because people looking in the correct category will never see your book and those in the wrong one will see it but have no interest. Imagine if you ran a department store and stocked Prada shoes in the hardware section.

Amazon has over 13,000 different categories spread out between books, eBooks, and Audio books. The odds of you being in the top ten or even number one are good.

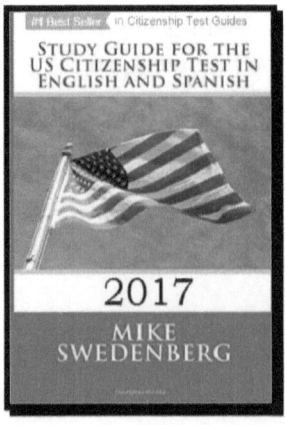

By being in the top 10 of a particular category, your book will show up on different Amazon pages and in the recommend buy list as well.

Rankings are fleeting. I'm constantly battling other study guides for the top ten spot. My English Spanish guide was number one for 8 months straight in 2016. Then another author took that spot and Amazon relegated me to the number two spot. The Amazon ranking stats are dynamic and fluctuate throughout the day. Check often.

I referred this to Dave Chesson, Kindle Marketing Jedi at Kindlepreneur.com who said, "Amazon doesn't do human checks. They use their algo (algorithm) to quickly see if there are any red flags about what the person claims upon publishing. If no red flags rise, then no human check. So you see things like that. The truth is, when trying to figure out Amazon and their decisions it really comes down to, 'What makes Amazon money.'"

Age Range

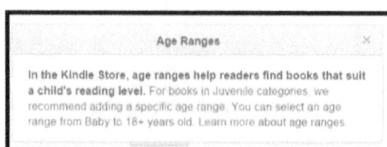

Children's books are divided into age groups according to average reading and attention spans.

According to Lisa Rojany Buccieri and Peter Economy in their book *Age Levels for Children's Books* – Wiley

Board books: Newborn to age 3

Picture books: Ages 3–8

Coloring and activity (C&A) books: Ages 3–8

Novelty books: Ages 3 and up, depending on content

Early, leveled readers: Ages 5–9

First chapter books: Ages 6–9 or 7–10

Middle-grade books: Ages 8–12

Young adult (YA) novels: Ages 12 and up or 14 and up

"It's okay to veer off a year or so in either direction when assigning a target audience age range to your work."

US Grade Range

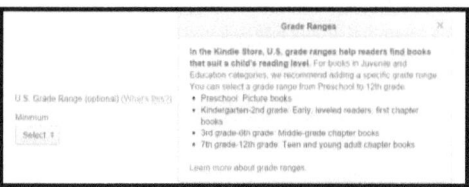

Grade ranges are easier to determine and used for Children's Books or those for Young Adults

Age 3-5 / Preschool

Kindergarten - 2nd grade

Early-level readers, first chapter books

3rd - 6th grade

Middle-grade chapter books

7th - 12th grade

Keywords, Release & Upload

Unless you want to release your book at a later date, choose NOW.

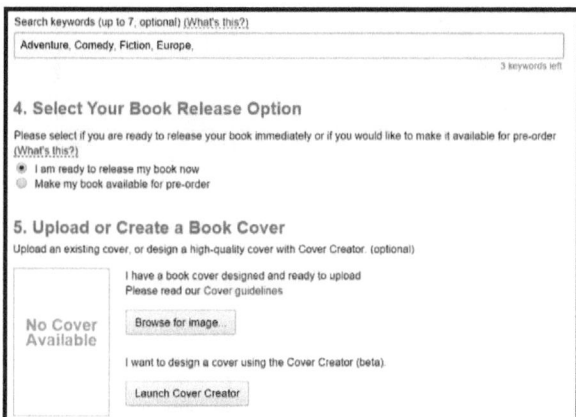

Upload book file and continue. You cannot use the same interior file with KDP Print as you do with Kindle.

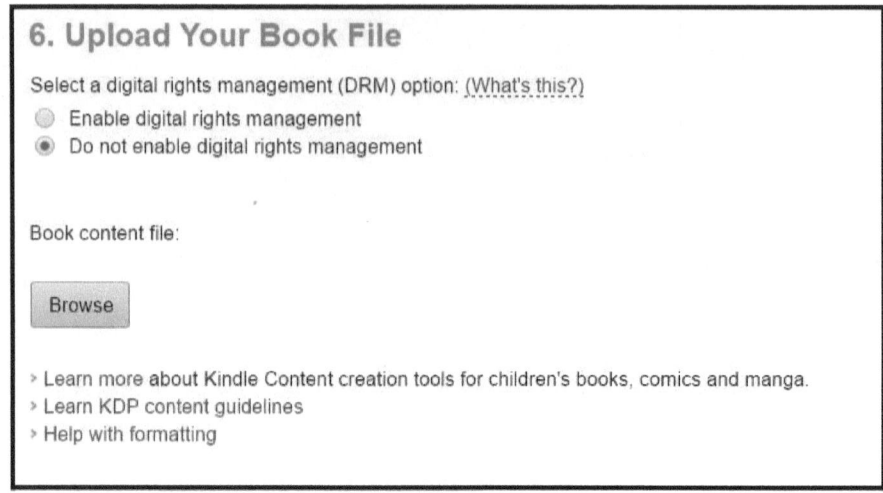

Choose worldwide rights unless there are countries you do not want your book published.

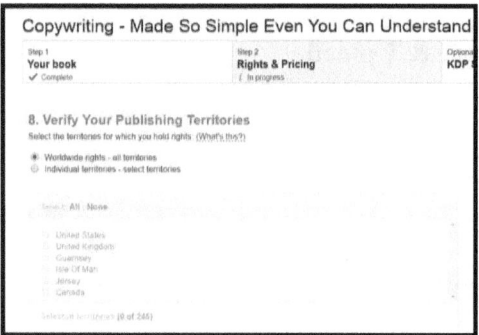

Analyze and Set price

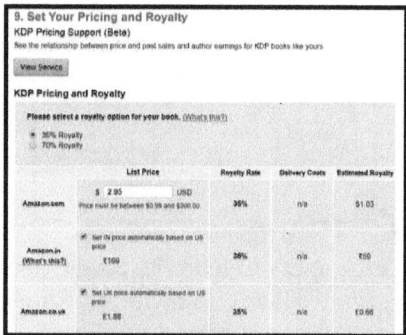

Click on view service. KDP has restrictions on where else you want your book. Currently, all of my Kindles are on KDP therefore I can choose 70% royalties.

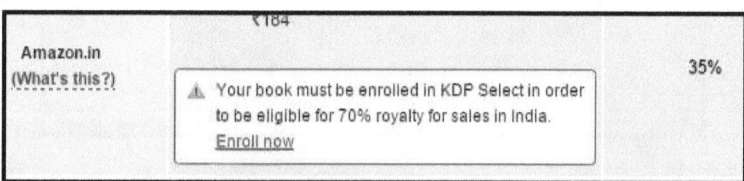

This chart represents the ideal price for an eBook. The best price is surprising $2.99.

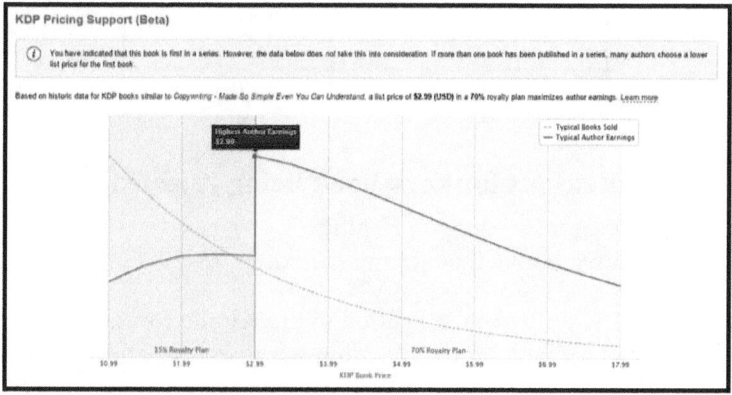

Matchbook and lending lets your customers purchase your e-book at a discount when they have purchased your book in print through CreateSpace.com.

Lending allows your customers to lend the ebook they bought from you to others for a limited time. This is no different from someone buying your print book and lending it to a friend. It gets you additional exposure and a recommendation. Who loans a book they didn't like themselves?

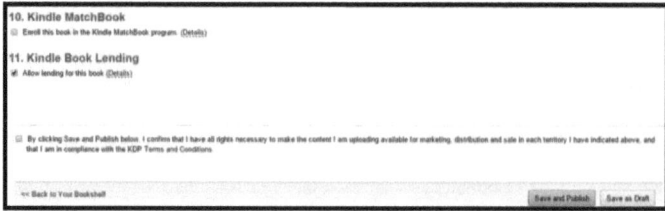

Reasons for your book being rejected

Content Unsuited for Reading on Kindle
Kindle will remove books that are not suited.

Some books are simply not well suited to the Kindle format. These include any kind of book where the main purpose is to allow the reader to write or color on the pages. These books are better suited to publishing in a physical form. Examples of books not suited to the Kindle format include the following:

Puzzle books

Blank Journals

Pattern books

Coloring books

Connect the Dots

Facing page translations (left page in one language, right page is same content in another language)

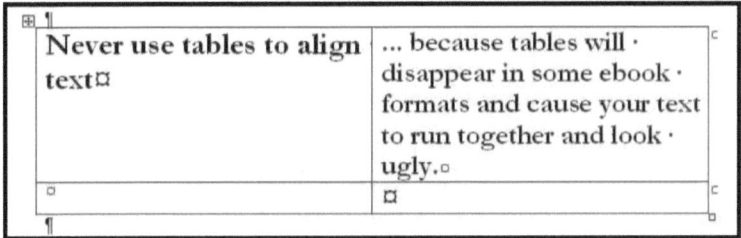

| Never use tables to align text | ... because tables will disappear in some ebook formats and cause your text to run together and look ugly. |

This is normal text. ·Note how it is not surrounded by the box. ·Normal text flows · freely across the page. ·Normal text converts well into multiple ebook formats.¶

My Published Writers

This is a partial list of my fellow writers who published their books after taking my classes. I wish to acknowledge their hard work and patience as they plowed through a myriad of technical and often times tedious process, but persevere they did.

I will update this book each year to reflect changes in the market and process along with more published works.

Your book will be added if you wish.

MY LUPUS JOURNEY is a story about the time Aimee was diagnosed with Lupus and how she weathered many trials and challenges on her journey of twenty years with the disease.
Aimee Ackell

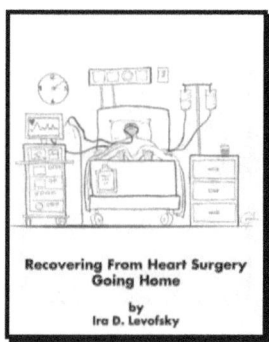

"What Mr.Ira Levofsky has done with this book based on his own life and experience with cardiac surgery is very special and will be of help to patients and their support network."
Dr. Daniel Goldman MD, FAAC, FHRS

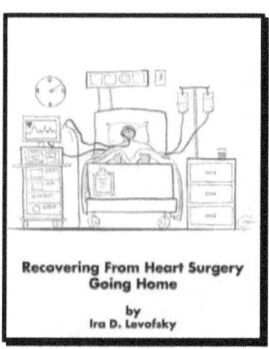

An innovative, in-depth system where the MLB playoff teams will be determined via democracy.
Peter Walton

Hoping she would have made Erma Bombeck proud, Nancy writes about her everyday life with an openness, wit and humor that keeps readers wanting more.
Nancy H. Lopez

The author draws upon the skills and knowledge she has gained and as well as the real-life experiences of her extended family, friends and co-workers to give men and women of all generations the tools, tips, insights and motivation to succeed.   Helen Fletschinger

MAKE THE MOST OF YOUR 20's! Your decisions will impact your
long-term health, finances, relationships, and fulfillment. With the
book's inspiring stories and "customize your life" activities, you're on
your way to a happier life
Irene Caniano

A retired teacher became the publisher of the "Beachcomber," a
community newspaper in New York City shortly before September 11,
2001 and had led his paper's coverage of the terrorist attack and the 75
locals who died in that attack. Now, his world literally fell in around him.
Howard J. Schwach

Index

About the Author

Mike Swedenberg has been publishing books for over ten years. He provides copywriting, coaching and teaches continuing education classes at Nassau Community College.

His educational background in business, sales, creative writing and marketing has given him a broad base from which to approach many topics.

His writing skills are confirmed independently on Amazon.com He especially enjoys producing study guides and self-help books.

Sam Chinkes
Las Vegas, NV.

Other books by the Author

A New York Wedding – a novel

Bully Boss – a novel

The Road Warrior a sales manual

Advertising Copywriting and the Unique Selling Proposition

Smart Money Stupid Money

21 ½ Things to Know Before Self-Publishing

How to Publish an eBook

Study Guide for the US Immigration Test in 14 languages

Notes:

_____

_____

_____

_____

_____

_____

_____

_____

_____

_____

_____

_____

_____

_____

_____

_____

_____

_____

_____

_____

_____

_____

_____

_____

_____

_____

_____

_____

_____

_____

_____

_____

_____

_____

_____

_____

_____

www.ingramcontent.com/pod-product-compliance
Lightning Source LLC
Chambersburg PA
CBHW021847170526
45157CB00007B/2978